Following the Moon

Also by James Norbury

Big Panda and Tiny Dragon

*The Journey: A Big Panda and
Tiny Dragon Adventure*

The Cat Who Taught Zen

Following the Moon

James Norbury

MICHAEL JOSEPH

For Ruth
You followed the moon with me.
Thank you.

Dawn

Winter had come to the mountains.

The great river ran deep and clear.

And of all the trees, only the pines kept their dark,
waxy needles.

Alone for the first time in her life,
Amaya wandered the silent landscape
in search of her parents.

For two days she travelled, her strength waning with every step,
until, one cloudless night, she thought she heard a sound
coming from the forest beyond.

Something she recognized.

Keeping low, Amaya approached until she could
see the source of it.

Relief flooded through her as she saw it was
just as she had hoped.

More dogs – larger than her mother and father
and with different patterns in their fur.

She felt a wave of excitement
and headed through the trees towards them.

As she approached, the nearest wolf snapped its head around,
yellow eyes bright in the darkness.

Without hesitation the creature leapt at Amaya,
its teeth tearing a chunk of fur from her back.

Amaya yelped and tried to run,
but another wolf cut her off.

And another, and another, until she was surrounded
by fierce eyes and bared teeth.

There was no way out.

She screwed up her eyes, hid under her paws and
waited for what she knew would come.

Barks and snarls echoed through the cold morning air.
Amaya had no idea what was happening,
but she was still alive.

She dared to peek with one eye, only to see that a single wolf,
bigger and older than the others, stood over her.

Although badly wounded, it seemed to be daring the pack
to try something, but all they did was slowly circle.

Then one attacked . . .

The big wolf grabbed Amaya in its teeth and ran.

Trees flew past them in the darkness.

She could hear the pack behind them,
but gradually their baying faded and the only sound
was the Wolf's panting and its paws drumming the snow.

The Wolf slowed to a stop and placed Amaya on the snowy ground.

She looked up at the creature.

It was wounded from the fight and panting hard.

Its face was laced with a lifetime of scars,
but she sensed a deep, still presence within it and was not afraid.

'Are you all right?' asked the Wolf.
Amaya nodded slowly. 'You saved me.'

'We need to find shelter,' said the Wolf.
'Come with me.'

Evening

The snow showed no signs of stopping,
and so Amaya and the Wolf sought refuge in a cave.

He had led his pack for almost a decade but the Wolf was now
badly wounded and no longer the creature he once was.

If he were to stay in the cave to rest, he might recover.

Maybe even one day return to the pack.

Yet the Wolf somehow knew this would never happen.

He still had no idea what had possessed him to save this small puppy;
all he knew was that it felt like the right thing to do.

Amaya walked out of the cave
and seated herself by the Wolf.

'Where are your parents?' asked the Wolf.

'I don't know,' said Amaya. 'We were separated in a storm.'

'Do you know which direction they might be?'
Amaya shook her head.

'To reach any destination,' said the Wolf,
'you need a direction – without knowing which way to travel,
we won't be able to find your parents.'

Amaya looked helplessly out to the horizon,
searching for an answer as to where they should go.
She was silent for a moment and then turned to the Wolf.
'My mother once told me a tale about the moon.'

The Wolf remained silent.

'She said that if you followed the moon, with all your heart,
it would take you where you needed to be.'

The Wolf snorted. 'That's nonsense.'

'Oh,' said Amaya, 'I . . .'

Seeing the puppy's face fall, the Wolf instantly regretted his words.
'But what would I know?' he said. 'Perhaps your mother was right.'

'Do you think so?' asked Amaya.

'I don't know,' said the Wolf.
'Following the moon may not achieve anything,
but staying here talking about it definitely won't.'

'But I don't know what lies in that direction,' said Amaya.
'It would be a journey into the unknown.'

A glint appeared in the Wolf's eye. 'That's my favourite kind.'

'We should start now,' said the Wolf,

'for the moon will not wait for us.'

'You never know when the clouds will come and
we'll wish we'd taken the chance while it was there.'

As they passed between the birches,
Amaya couldn't help but notice the Wolf
was limping and his breathing was laboured.

'Are you all right?' she asked.

The Wolf was not all right, he could feel the life ebbing from his body.

But despite this, he knew this was the path he must take.
He had never wanted anything so much
as to protect this innocent creature's dream.

'My form is breaking,' said the Wolf,
'but I feel as though something inside me is changing
and growing stronger.'

Amaya looked into the old Wolf's eyes.
'Are you sure? We could rest more.'

'No,' said the Wolf.

'The path ahead is perhaps the most difficult one I will ever travel.
But I will embrace it, I will devote myself fully to it,
and I will welcome every trial that it brings,
for I know it is what I need to take me where I need to be.

'Come,' he said, gathering his strength.

'Everything that is important will happen today.'

'What do you mean?' asked Amaya.

'There is no tomorrow,' said the Wolf,
'tomorrow – when it matters – will be today.'

They continued through the forest,
the moon high and bright above them.

But as the forest thinned, their way was blocked by
a towering cliff stretching away to either side
as far as they could see.

With no means to scale it, the Wolf turned to his right and
began to follow the cliff.

'Is this the best way?' asked Amaya,
seeing that they were no longer heading
in the direction of the moon.

The Wolf nodded. 'Yes, Amaya.
For now, we are forced to head in a new direction,
but everything before us is still the way.

No matter the twists and turns, the trials and the obstacles,
it is always the way – the path.

You cannot walk another one ...

So we must have faith and give this one everything we have.'

Before long, they came across a deep fissure leading into the rock.
Beyond, Amaya could just make out shaped stones, pillars and stairs.

'This may take us back towards the moon,' said the Wolf.

Amaya was not sure, but as the Wolf had just said,
this was now the path. She certainly did not want to be alone again,
so ran to catch up with the Wolf.

Midnight

The passage opened out into a maze of ancient,
ruined buildings.

But to Amaya's excitement, she could see that by
following a series of winding stone steps,
they would once more be on the trail of the moon.

When they reached the surface,
before them rose the ruins of a city.
Its streets were flooded, reflecting the moon in its dark, still waters.

Amaya noticed the fresh wounds on the Wolf's body, still wet
in the moonlight, and her mind was drawn back to the fight.

'Who were those other wolves?' asked Amaya.

'They were my pack,' said the Wolf, 'my friends for many years.
They helped to make me who I am and I owe them a great deal.'

Amaya looked confused.

'Well . . .' said the Wolf, 'you see the moon?
Did you know, it has no light of its own,
it can only reflect the light of the sun.

But the moon is at peace with this,
and just as beautiful as the sun.'

'What does the moon do for the sun?' asked Amaya.

'It tells her of the stars and how the world looks
under the veil of moonlight.'

Amaya smiled. 'They are both very lucky.'

'They are,' agreed the Wolf,
'because they have chosen to give to one another.'

'Do you see those flowers growing in that dark corner?'
asked the Wolf.

'Without the fireflies, we wouldn't be able to see them.
Sometimes it's the presence of another that lets us shine.

If you remember this, Amaya, it will help you to not resent it
when another thrives, but to welcome it and be glad for them.

Another's gifts might be just what we need to unlock our own.'

'Then why were you fighting the rest of your pack?' asked Amaya.

'If I'm honest, I don't know.
I took you and ran. It seemed like the right thing to do.'

'Do you regret it?' asked Amaya.

'No, despite our current situation,
I have never been more sure of anything.'

The Wolf looked up to the night sky,
feelings stirring in him that he'd long forgotten.
'We are here . . . now . . . this is my life,
unfolding before me, beneath the great moon.'

A freezing wind blew in from the north and
the snow turned into wet, icy sleet.

'Come,' said the Wolf, 'we should find some shelter.'

In the safety of an abandoned observatory, the Wolf and Amaya
sat together watching the storm.

The walls around them were painted with peeling murals depicting
the moon and its passage across the heavens. It seems it had long
fascinated those who had built this strange structure.

Amaya wondered if in the past others had tried to follow the moon.

All of a sudden she was struck by a thought that perhaps she
was being naive to think she could follow the moon, that her quest was
dangerous and foolish, and that the Wolf knew this.

'Thank you for coming on this journey with me,' said Amaya.

The Wolf turned to her, and for the first time she saw his face
soften into a smile.

'The greatest journeys are the ones we take with others,' he replied.

The storm fell to a whisper and the companions left the observatory, following a winding cobbled path that led down the hillside and into a dark wood.

Amaya approached cautiously. She couldn't make out anything within the black depths of the trees. 'It's very dark in there.'

'It is our path,' said the Wolf.

Amaya remembered what he had said about not just following the path, not just accepting it, but embracing it, no matter the hardships.

'It is,' said Amaya, walking towards the darkness.

But the strangest thing was, as she entered the forest,
the darkness she had seen from the outside was nowhere
to be seen.

Once within the trees she could see everything . . .
and it was wondrous.

'It was just an illusion,' said the Wolf.
'When we bring the light of our presence to something,
there is little we cannot understand.

And as we begin to understand, our fear,
like the darkness, begins to fade.'

The first streaks of light brushed the sky.

Dawn

Ahead, Amaya could see strange dancing lights.

As they got closer, she saw fireflies circling the most enchanting pond.

'Incredible,' said Amaya, taking in all the flowers.

'And how amazing that they grow here in the depths of this wood, hidden from the sun.'

'This one is a lotus flower,' said the Wolf.
'Its roots travel down through the water into the mud
at the bottom of the pond.

And although they begin their lives in the dark and the filth,
their flowers rise above the black waters,
glorious and beautiful, reaching for the heavens.'

Amaya looked a little forlorn. 'I don't think I can be like the lotus.'

'Why do you say that?' asked the Wolf.

'I've lost my mother and father, and although you are helping me,
I wonder if I will ever find them.
I cannot imagine things will go well for me.'

'The reason the lotus blooms,' said the Wolf,
'is because it just keeps going – the little shoot has no idea
how deep the pond is, how far it needs to climb or what
might be in its way, it just keeps going.

And the fact that it started from a very dark place
doesn't stop it.'

'So, you really think there's a chance to find my parents?'
asked Amaya.

'Not if we stop trying.'

'But what if we're going in the wrong direction?'

'Perhaps we are, but we are doing what we can based
on what we think is best.

If we learn something new, we can walk a new path.
Until then – we should continue to follow the moon.

And don't forget, your mother said, "With all your heart".

I think she knew what she was talking about.'

They journeyed on, the moon still just visible in the dawn sky.
Before long the forest gave way, once more, to the forgotten city.

'This place is so magical,' said Amaya.
'When my mother saw things such as this, she would write
a poem or a song. I thought about doing that – but I
wouldn't be good at that sort of thing.'

'How do you know if you've never done it?'
asked the Wolf.

'You know, somewhere inside you is a poem
that you alone can write. A unique blend of what you love,
what you fear and all the things that only you
have experienced.

That is the poem to write, young one.'

'But what if others don't like it?'

'Perhaps no one will like it, Amaya, not even you,
and that's okay. That is why we need to take our joy
in the creation, not how it turns out.

And when you write your poem, Amaya, take your time
choosing a place to sit and a subject that inspires you.

Enjoy searching for the right words, even if it takes all day.
Relish the way the world changes around you as you create.

The result is really beyond our control.

If we are only concerned about how it turns out
and what others might think,
we have lost that which makes creation joyous.'

The Wolf's own words struck him hard,
and he knew he was rediscovering something he had lost.

Morning

With morning came hope.

As the sun broke across the mountains, Amaya's heart leapt.

'This house. . .' she said, 'I remember it.
I am sure we stayed here one night during a storm.'

'Then we are on the right path,' said the Wolf,
'let's hurry while we can still see the moon.'

The trail followed the river into a steep-sided gorge.

But as they rounded a bend in the path, Amaya's heart sank.

A great waterfall blocked their path.
Normally they could have passed beneath it,
but the winter air had frozen the water solid,
cutting off any hope of continuing this way.

'Will we have to go back?' asked Amaya.
'Will we be able to find another way?'

'I have been watching you,'
said a voice from somewhere above them.

Amaya and the Wolf looked up to see a cat, seated on a rock.

'Do you always travel so slowly?' asked the Cat.

'Yes, we do,' said Amaya confidently.
'But as long as we don't stop, we'll get where we're going.'

'And where is that?' asked the Cat.

'To find my parents,' said Amaya. 'We're following the moon.'

The Cat smiled knowingly and looked to the moon,
which was now barely visible in the morning sky.

'What a good idea,' he said.

'So, what should we do?' asked Amaya.
'Do you know another route around?'

'I am enjoying the view,' said the Cat.
'I've never seen a frozen waterfall.
Stay with me and savour it.'

'We can't,' said Amaya, 'the moon is nearly gone and it's
the only way I can find my mother and father.'

The cat lay down in a patch of sunlight.

'Unless you can climb like a cat,
I don't know of another route.

Come, sit and enjoy the world.'

Amaya looked to the Wolf, who shrugged and settled down.

'Surely we should do something?' said Amaya.
'Chip at the ice perhaps.'

'There are times,' said the Cat,
'when we have done everything we can do.
Then we must learn to step back and allow the universe
to play out in all its unfathomable wonder.'

Amaya thought back to the Wolf's words.

I will embrace it, I will devote myself fully to it,
and I will welcome every trial that it brings.

This was just a different kind of trial, one that required nothing
of her but to allow things to be.

She realized that sometimes doing nothing was harder than
doing something.

So, she lay down to watch the sun rise over the gorge,
and as it did, her mind began to quiet and her worries faded.

The rising sun shone on cat, wolf and dog alike,
but unknown to Amaya, it was also bathing the
waterfall in warm morning sunlight.

An earsplitting crash shook Amaya from her peace.

Spinning round, she saw the frozen waterfall behind them
had broken away from the cliff and was crashing to the ground,
exploding into a shower of snow and ice.

But the way ahead was now clear.

The Cat smiled.

'Thanks to impermanence, all things are possible.'

Noon

So, they left the Cat to his musings and continued their journey.

The passage beneath the waterfall opened out into a set of stone steps
that wound its way through yet more crumbling ruins.

Suddenly Amaya stopped, her eyes to the sky.

'It's gone,' she whispered.

The Wolf looked at her questioningly.
'The moon . . . It's gone.'

'Well, of course,' said the Wolf,
'the moon hides her face in the daylight.'

'Then how will we continue our search?'

'We cannot rely on something being there forever,'
said the Wolf.

'Much like the Cat said, all things are impermanent,
both the good and the bad.

Just because we have lost sight of our goal,
it doesn't mean we should give up.

There is always the possibility of a new way.'

'But I don't want a new way,' said Amaya.
'The moon has led us where we need to be.
It can't leave us now.'

Amaya hung her head.

The Wolf looked at the little dog, lost and without hope.

Her parents were gone, the moon had left her,
and he knew in his heart that his body was failing
by the hour.

By the end of the day he would leave her too.

But that had not happened.
That was still in the future, and right now,
he wanted to use his last hours in the best way he could.

'When you said the moon had led us where we needed to be,
you were more right than you knew,' said the Wolf.

'The moon has led us exactly where we need to be.

Here.
Now.
Together.

Facing this challenge.'

'You know,' said the Wolf, looking up at the midday sun.
'My mother used to tell me something too.

She said, if you walked in the sunlight, luck would walk with you.'

Amaya looked suspicious. 'Really?'

The Wolf nodded in what he hoped was an earnest manner.

Amaya raised an eyebrow.

'Well, I suppose it's better than nothing.'

So, she looked about her for where the sunlight fell strongest.
'This way?' she asked.

'I would say so,' said the Wolf.

They walked across a great bridge that led past
ancient leaning towers.

Amaya was careful to keep an eye on the shadows
and follow the sunlight.

'You know,' she said to the Wolf, 'I thought journeys
were all about getting somewhere and having a destination,
but ours doesn't have one. It was all about the idea,
but when the moon disappeared, I felt so empty.'

'You still had a goal, Amaya, something you were working towards,
and that's no bad thing, but most of our lives are spent doing the travelling,
and the arrival is only a tiny part of that journey.

We should do our best to enjoy every part of the adventure.
Maybe we will never get where we want to be,
and wouldn't it be sad if we had not even enjoyed the ride?'

'How do I do that?' asked Amaya.

'Slow down, look around, breathe, take in the sounds and colours.
Imagine you'd chosen this moment as your destination,
not just a point along your journey.'

Amaya nodded.
'I can try that.'

Afternoon

The climb was unforgiving and both companions were soon exhausted.

'I don't think we should go on,' said Amaya,
looking at the path ahead.

'We have no idea where we're going, we have no moon,
and even the sun is hiding behind the mountain.'

The Wolf stopped and turned to the little dog.

'We cannot stop, Amaya. Just because we can't see something, it doesn't mean it's gone. Just as you said, the sun is hiding, but you know it's still there.'

Amaya huffed. 'It's not the same.'

The Wolf sighed; he was weak and this climb felt beyond him.

Common sense would have told him to stay back in the cave, to live out his last hours in peace, not struggling up the side of a freezing mountain.

He paused for a moment – the words did not come easily to him.
'We should carry on for each other, Amaya.

Protecting you is the only thing I have done that truly makes sense
to me and I want to see you back with your family.

So please, let's keep going.'

'But I thought you were coming along for me,'
said Amaya.

'I was,' said the Wolf,
'but now I ask you to come along for me.'

The little dog thought back to what the Wolf had said
back outside the cave, she then stood up and shook the
snow from her fur and starting walking.

'Come on then, Mr Wolf,
you never know when the clouds will come and
we'll wish we had taken the chance while it was there.'

The Wolf struggled to stand.
His legs were weak and sore and
his fur did little to keep out the icy wind.

And then he realized that this was the last time
he would experience these things.
The last time he would feel the touch of cold
as a snowflake landed on his nose.

The last time he would see the broken clouds,
luminous with the day's fading light. Never again
would he awaken to a new morning or make a new friend.
The enormity of it welled up within him.

So, what was there to do but intently live every second
and embrace the path that was laid out before him.

This stark realization made him intensely aware of the
world around him, and he wished, for a moment,
that he had always had the capacity to witness such beauty.

Doing his best to ignore the pain, he caught up to Amaya.

'Do you see that?' asked the Wolf, looking up.

Amaya followed his gaze, and there, high above them,
faint but unmistakable,
was the moon.

Dusk

'It came back,' said Amaya, smiling. 'We can follow it again.'

'Yes,' said the Wolf. 'We were lucky.
But imagine if it hadn't.'

Again Amaya looked confused.
'Then what would we have done?'

'We adapt, we change, we find a new way forward.
There is nothing wrong with acknowledging that a path is not
leading us where we need to be and choosing a new one.'

'But what if none of the plans had worked?' asked Amaya.

'Sometimes it's simply not possible
to try hard and get the result we want.
Imagine digging up a seed to see whether it had grown.
If we've watered it, there really is nothing left to do.

No matter how hard we try,
we cannot MAKE the moon appear.'

The Wolf was tired and struggled
to hold his thoughts together.

He settled down into the snow for the last time.

'We had faith, Amaya, we kept going and hopefully you will be rewarded – I know I have been.

But it's important to remember, sometimes we are not rewarded, sometimes our struggles and patience and optimism will be for nothing. But the journey itself, how we did it, and who we did it with, will always live within us.

That's why we do things with all our heart,
so when it doesn't work out, at least
we know we put the best of ourselves into the world.'

The Wolf watched Amaya.
He knew that she would have to continue the search
for her parents alone.

It pained him more than he could have ever imagined.

But as he was just telling her, it did not matter how much
he wanted to help her, guide her and protect her – some things
were beyond his control.

He wanted to explain.

The Wolf's breathing slowed.

He thought back to his time as a cub, a parent,
a loyal ally and a fierce enemy.

He'd led the pack to great victories and bitter defeats.

His life was a tapestry of successes and failures,
and he wondered what different choices he could have made
that would have saved him from dying on this mountain top,
exiled from his pack.

Then he looked at Amaya, staring up at the moon,
and he knew that everything was exactly as it should be.

'Every time I watch the moon,' said the Wolf,
'I always notice something different.'

The Wolf felt whole.
His life complete in every way.

'Does following the moon REALLY work?'
asked Amaya.

The Wolf took a moment to think back over
their journey together.

'I don't know,' he said,
'but consider this.'

'We did something, Amaya.
For ourselves, and more importantly, for each other.
You gave me something I did not even know I was missing.
And I hope I have helped you.'

'And when you look up at the moon,' said the Wolf,
'you will always be able to look back on this time we have spent together
and remember when we threw common sense to the wind
and followed something which cannot be followed.

You will remember all the things we spoke of,
the discoveries, the successes,
the feelings of loss and disappointment.

And you'll know that when everything seems to be falling apart
and you feel like you've lost your way,
just have a little faith, stay strong,
keep searching, and you might just find your way again.'

'I'm sorry, Amaya, I am so very tired – I must sleep.'

And the Wolf curled into the snow beneath the full moon
and left the world.

His slow breaths giving way to the silent dusk.

A stillness hung in the winter forest.

Amaya felt a change in the air –
she approached the Wolf and touched his nose with hers.

Something was different.
Something was missing.

The Wolf was there, his grey fur stirring in the wind,
but she could no longer sense his spirit.

He was gone,
and she was alone in the world once more.

She pressed herself into the Wolf's
fur and sought comfort in his lingering warmth.

Night

Hours passed . . .

Amaya woke to a midnight moon.

And she remembered what had happened.
She looked at the Wolf and wondered where he was now.

But as the air stirred and clouds broke,
she knew he was all around her . . .

His howl was echoed in the wind
that moved between the trees.

His form ran forever free among the stars.

His ageless soul would always live deep in the mountains
he called home.

But most of all, even if she travelled to a distant land
where the wind didn't blow, the stars didn't shine
and no mountains touched the sky,
the Wolf would never leave her heart.

Amaya looked up into the night sky,
at the great moon hanging in the darkness.

And she realized what the whole journey had been about.

The search for her parents, the Wolf's decision to save her,
leaving the safety of the cave and following the moon.

It was about love.

And although Amaya was by herself,
she did not feel abandoned.

Alone

The snow began to fall once more.

She was here again.

Alone.

Lost.

But this time it was different.

She had known the Wolf for such a very short time,
but the love he had shown her had affected her profoundly.

Amaya searched the sky for the moon and chose
the path which best followed it.

She took one last look at her friend, at peace among the trees,
and began walking – for this was now the path.

She walked for many miles and still
saw no sign of anything she recognized.

And although she still felt the Wolf's presence,
she wished he really was with her now.
His thick grey fur catching the snowflakes,
his big paws leaving huge prints in the snow.

She hadn't realized how close she had grown to him in
such a short time, and his death had left a hollow in her heart.

The journey seemed so much harder without
someone to share it with.

She had been travelling for many hours when she heard
a quiet crying coming from somewhere up ahead.

Cautiously, Amaya approached.

She dug at the snow and there,
sheltering in the hollow of a tree, was a kitten.

It looked up at Amaya with wide eyes.

'Hello.'

'What are you doing out here?' asked Amaya.
'This is no place for a kitten.'
The kitten looked down forlornly.

'I don't know. I was chasing snowflakes with
my brothers and when I turned round,
I was alone. I searched and searched but
just seemed to get more and more lost.'

Amaya crawled under the fallen tree and
shared her warmth with the tiny kitten.

'I was also lost,' she said.

'I became separated from my parents
but while looking for them,
I had the most incredible encounter.'

And Amaya told a tale of an old Wolf and
a winter forest, a ruined city and a guiding moon.

The snow fell softly and the kitten listened.

And as she told her story, it became even more clear
to Amaya how much the Wolf had changed her world
in such a short time.

She could help the kitten, but what if
that meant there would come a time when
she might have to abandon her own search?

Amaya thought back to the Wolf and felt a great
sense of strength and purpose, and she realized
that it was a sacrifice she was prepared to make.

'We are both lost,' said Amaya,
'but now we can follow the moon together.
It will take us where we need to be.'

'How do we follow the moon?'
asked the kitten.

'With all our heart,' said Amaya.
'It's the only way that works.'

THE END

. . . and the beginning.

AFTERWORD

I've been a cautious person most of my life, mostly due to a lack of money. I was always scared of losing my home or not being able to pay vet bills, etc. Saying that, I could be considered rather foolish as I insisted that I could earn my living with art and writing. I was terrible at selling my work, but I had my moon and I followed it. I prepared for a worst-case scenario and then I went for it.

Of course, things did work out for me eventually, but it did take twenty-five years to get there. And, as I am sure we're all aware, being successful in your job is no guarantee of a fulfilled life.

I was asked by an interviewer a few weeks back what advice I would give to teenage James, and after much thought, I decided I would keep my mouth shut. Because the journey I took – with its heart-wrenching lows and life-changing highs – I would not change for anything.

But surely – I spent twenty-five years with very little money, I lost people I cared about, I have been depressed, anxious, defeated, addicted, and at one point completely gave up trying to do anything creative – surely, I would change some of those things?

No, not one.

'. . . this is my life, unfolding before me, beneath the great moon.'

Every piece is part of the whole, and who knows what taking one of those components (however awful) away would change? It takes a great deal of perspective to see that the pain and suffering are intrinsic and necessary to the journey, but I believe they are and that in knowing this, we can attempt to embrace such hardships and hopefully learn to be a little more accepting of them.

Following the Moon was a very difficult book for me as it was based purely on instinct and was something I felt I needed to write. It delves deep into things that caused me great emotional upheaval, and at times was simply painful, but coming out the other side, I am so pleased I was given the opportunity to create it. I am sure the book, as I initially proposed it, was not the most attractive package for my publisher, but my editor willingly climbed aboard my crazy boat and off we sailed together.

I hope that in reading this book you are inspired to follow your own moon, or if you're already following it, not to give up. Because even if we never get where we intended, there is a wealth of experiences to be had along the way, and it is these experiences (good and bad) which allow us to shape ourselves. When viewed in this way, we can start to see the potential in everything that happens to us, and just maybe we can start to enjoy each day a little more.

23/8/23

ACKNOWLEDGEMENTS

Dan – Nothing I can write is sufficient, so you'll have to make do with these crude words. Thank you for your endless support and vision. Your heart is inspiring.

Ruth – How many moons have we chased? How many did we catch? It doesn't matter, because we love the game, unfair as it often seems.

Martyn – I am sorry for my demented ramblings. Thank you so much for your ideas. I will never forget your droplets of rain on the car bonnet. You're a magician.

Hannah – You hold the demons at the gate. It makes a huge difference. I wish everyone could have a Hannah. Thank you.

Ludo – Thank you again for all the work you do behind the scenes allowing me to focus on what's important.

The Wolf – I miss you. Thank you.

FINAL WORD

While writing page 127, I received a message from a neighbour to say our cat, Philip, was dead on the pavement outside. He was a young rescue cat with one eye (another cat had slashed the other).

We went out to collect him and wrapped him in a blanket, but due to factors, we could not bury him until the next day.

I am terribly fond of my cat friends, and I was deeply upset. I was angry at first (who had hit him with their car?), but over the course of the day, as I came back to visit his still-perfect form, I softened and just missed him. I kept expecting him to wake up.

The next morning, I was able to dig him a grave in our small garden.

I was also very conscious that I was writing a book in which death was one of the main themes, and I wondered how the ideas I had covered in the book applied to me now – face to face with the loss of a life I cared dearly for.

But as I laid him in the ground and covered him over, I knew that he wasn't really gone. I can still see him climbing over the walls, curled up in his favourite chair and jumping into the middle of the watercolour you can see on page 125 (nearly ruining it).

When I go into the garden he'll be there, I can talk to him. He'll be a good listener, I imagine.

I am, again, moved to tears as I write this – no one can take away the hurt of loss, but it is my sincere hope that when you do experience it, this book may offer some small solace.

Doing something with all your heart turns the meaningless into the meaningful.

'I think,' said the Wolf, 'that doing anything with all your heart might just take you where you need to be.'

MICHAEL JOSEPH

UK | USA | Canada | Ireland | Australia
India | New Zealand | South Africa

Michael Joseph is part of the Penguin
Random House group of companies
whose addresses can be found at
global.penguinrandomhouse.com.

Penguin
Random House
UK

First published in Great Britain by
Michael Joseph, 2024
001

Text copyright © James Norbury, 2024
Illustration copyright © James Norbury, 2024

The moral right of the author has been asserted

Set in Bauer Bellefair

Colour origination by Altaimage, London
Printed and bound in Germany by Mohn Media GmbH

A CIP catalogue record for this book is
available from the British Library

ISBN: 978-0-241-68673-7

www.greenpenguin.co.uk

MIX
Paper | Supporting
responsible forestry
FSC® C018179

Penguin Random House is committed to a
sustainable future for our business, our readers
and our planet. This book is made from Forest
Stewardship Council® certified paper.